NATURE'S GROSSEST

DOGS LICK THEIR BUTTS!

By Natalie Humphrey

Please visit our website, www.garethstevens.com. For a free color catalog of all our high-quality books, call toll free 1-800-542-2595 or fax 1-877-542-2596.

Cataloging-in-Publication Data
Names: Humphrey, Natalie.
Title: Dogs lick their butts! / Natalie Humphrey.
Description: New York : Gareth Stevens Publishing, 2024. | Series: Nature's grossest | Includes glossary and index.
Identifiers: ISBN 9781538285657 (pbk.) | ISBN 9781538285664 (library bound) | ISBN 9781538285671 (ebook)
Subjects: LCSH: Dogs–Health–Juvenile literature. | Dogs–Behavior–Juvenile literature.
Classification: LCC SF427.H86 2024 | DDC 636.7–dc23

Published in 2024 by
Gareth Stevens Publishing
2544 Clinton Street
Buffalo, NY 14224

Copyright © 2024 Gareth Stevens Publishing

Designer: Leslie Taylor
Editor: Natalie Humphrey

Photo credits: Series art (background) Oleksii Natykach/Shutterstock.com; cover Fcikle/Shutterstock.com; p. 5 Natalia Fedosova/Shutterstock.com; p. 7 Dora Zett/Shutterstock.com; p. 9 Masarik/Shutterstock.com; p. 11 Vincent Scherer/Shutterstock.com; p. 13 Anna Hoychuk/Shutterstock.com; p. 15 kobkik/Shutterstock.com; p. 17 Alex Zotov/Shutterstock.com; p. 19 Pressmaster/Shutterstock.com; p. 21 Rob Hainer/Shutterstock.com.

All rights reserved. No part of this book may be reproduced in any form without permission in writing from the publisher, except by a reviewer.

Printed in the United States of America

CPSIA compliance information: Batch #CSGS24: For further information contact Gareth Stevens at 1-800-542-2595.

Find us on

CONTENTS

Boldface words appear in the glossary.

Dogs Are Gross!

Dogs make great friends, but they have a lot of gross **habits**! Every dog owner has stories about their furry friends eating gross things they shouldn't or rubbing their butts on the floor. Can dogs be any more gross? You bet! Dogs lick their butts!

Different Kinds of Dogs

There are many different kinds of dogs. Some dogs have long coats, and others don't have fur at all! There are over 76 million pet dogs in the United States. No matter the kind of dog, they all lick their butts!

Taking Care of Dogs

Taking care of a dog is a lot of hard work! Dogs need to be **regularly** walked and fed, but **grooming** is also important. Dogs with long coats need to be washed and brushed more than dogs with shorter fur.

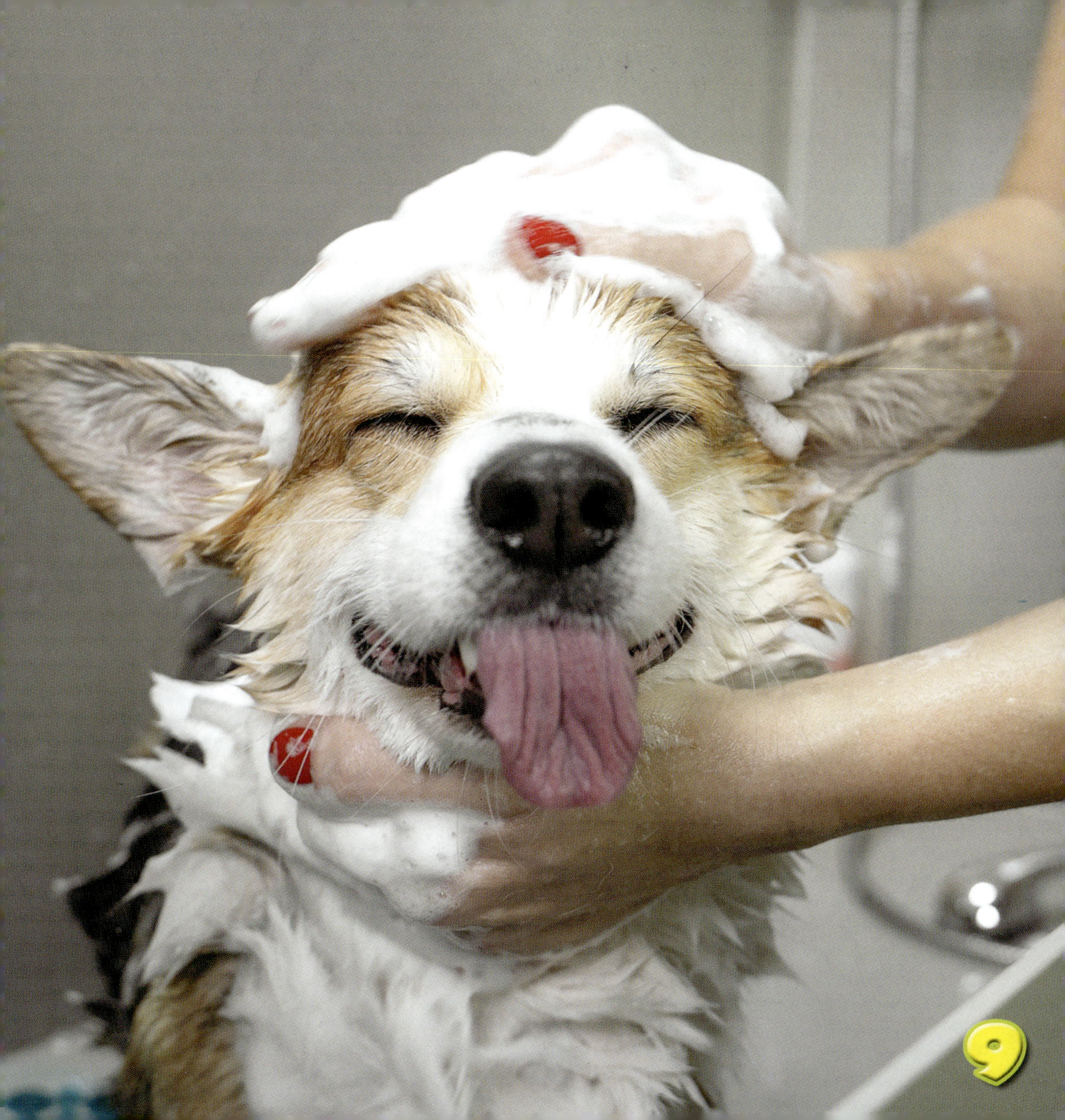

Why Do They Do That?

So why do clean dogs still lick their butts? Sometimes, dogs lick themselves to do some extra cleaning. If a dog feels like it isn't quite clean enough, they'll lick anywhere and everywhere on their bodies, including their butts!

Keeping Puppies Clean

Sometimes, a dog will even lick another dog's butt! Mother dogs will often lick their puppies to keep them clean. Licking their butts also helps **encourage** them to poop. Some dogs lick other dogs' butts just to be friendly. Yuck!

Dog Allergies

Dogs don't just lick their butts to stay clean. It might be a sign of trouble. Just like people, dogs can have **allergies**. If a dog is allergic to something they're eating or in their home, they may lick themselves nonstop!

Stinky Butts

Dogs have special **glands** inside of their bums that help them mark their **territory**. Sometimes, dogs need to lick their butts to keep these glands clean. If a dog's butt gets really stinky, the dog might start licking its butt!

Icky Problems

A dog might also lick their butt if they have something living inside of them. If a **parasite** made its home in a dog's belly, that dog might not feel very good. This makes the dog lick its butt!

Tell an Adult!

Even if it's gross, a dog licking its butt usually isn't a problem at all. But it's always important to keep a close eye on your furry friend. If you think something might be wrong, make sure to tell an adult!

GLOSSARY

allergy: A body's sensitivity to usually harmless things in the surroundings, such as dust, pollen, or mold.

encourage: To help make something happen.

gland: A body part that produces something needed for a bodily function.

grooming: The process of cleaning the fur, skin, or feathers.

habit: A set pattern of behavior that is repeated without thinking about it.

parasite: A living thing that lives in, on, or with another living thing and often harms it.

regularly: To do the same thing very often.

territory: An area of land that an animal considers to be its own and will fight to defend.

FOR MORE INFORMATION

BOOKS

Nugent, Samantha. *Dog*. New York, NY: AV2, 2022.

Peters, Katie. *I Care for My Pet*. Minneapolis, MN: Lerner Publications, 2023.

WEBSITES

Britannica Kids
kids.britannica.com/kids/article/dog/353060
Check out pictures, watch videos, and learn more fun facts about dogs!

National Georgraphic Kids
www.natgeokids.com/uk/discover/animals/general-animals/dog-facts/
Learn more about dogs and what makes them such great pets!

Publisher's note to educators and parents: Our editors have carefully reviewed these websites to ensure that they are suitable for students. Many websites change frequently, however, and we cannot guarantee that a site's future contents will continue to meet our high standards of quality and educational value. Be advised that students should be closely supervised whenever they access the Internet.

INDEX